THE *FANTASTIC* BOOK OF
Snow-
BOARDING

LESLEY McKENNA

COPPER BEECH BOOKS
BROOKFIELD, CONNECTICUT

© Aladdin Books Ltd 1998
© U.S. text 1998

*Designed and
produced by*
Aladdin Books Ltd
28 Percy Street
London W1P 0LD

*First published in the United States
in 1998 by*
Copper Beech Books,
an imprint of
The Millbrook Press
2 Old New Milford Road
Brookfield, Connecticut 06804

Editor
Sarah Levete
Design
David West
Children's Book Design
Designer
Flick Killerby
Illustrators
Richard Rockwood
Catherine Ward – Simon Girling &
Associates
Picture Research
Brooks Krikler Research

Printed in Belgium

Library of Congress
Cataloging-in-Publication Data
McKenna, Lesley.
Snowboarding / by Lesley McKenna ;
illustrated by Catherine Ward
and Richard Rockwood
p. cm. — (The fantastic book of—)
Includes index.
Summary: Provides step-by-step instructions
for both basic techniques and more advanced
tricks to be used in snowboarding.
ISBN 0-7613-0649-8 (trade : hc).
— ISBN 0-7613-0717-6 (lib. bdg.)
1. Snowboarding—Juvenile literature.
[1. Snowboarding.] I. Ward, Catherine, ill.
II. Rockwood, Richard, ill.
III. Title. IV. Series.
GV857.S57M366 1998   97-35115
796.9—dc21   CIP AC
5 4 3 2 1

CONTENTS

THE FOLD-OUT SECTION

Introduction

Snowboarding is fun, fast, and demanding. Whatever your age, whatever your ability, snowboarding has something to offer you. Read on, board up, and hit the snow.

Originally invented over twenty years ago by some surfers, snowboarding is now the fastest-growing winter sport — but you can do it during the summer, too! In snowboarding's early days, boarders were not allowed on the hills of ski resorts, but today many resorts encourage and welcome boarders.

Snowboarding is not just a sport, it's a way of life, too, influencing the fashion and music of today. Like other "extreme" sports, such as skateboarding and in-line skating, snowboarding is continually developing, as riders discover new and exciting challenges (*right*).

Snowboarding can be dangerous — you need to be very aware of safety, at all times. Begin with some lessons with a qualified instructor on a smaller, uncrowded ski slope.

Whether or not you are an experienced rider, this book tells you everything you need to know about snowboarding, from putting on your bindings to "catching some air," or jumping.

An eight-page fold-out goes behind the scenes at a top-level snowboarding competition, showing you what's involved, from training to helicopter drops.

As long as you are fit and healthy, you can enjoy the freedom and challenge of snowboarding. Whatever you do, and whatever your level, stay safe and have fun!

4

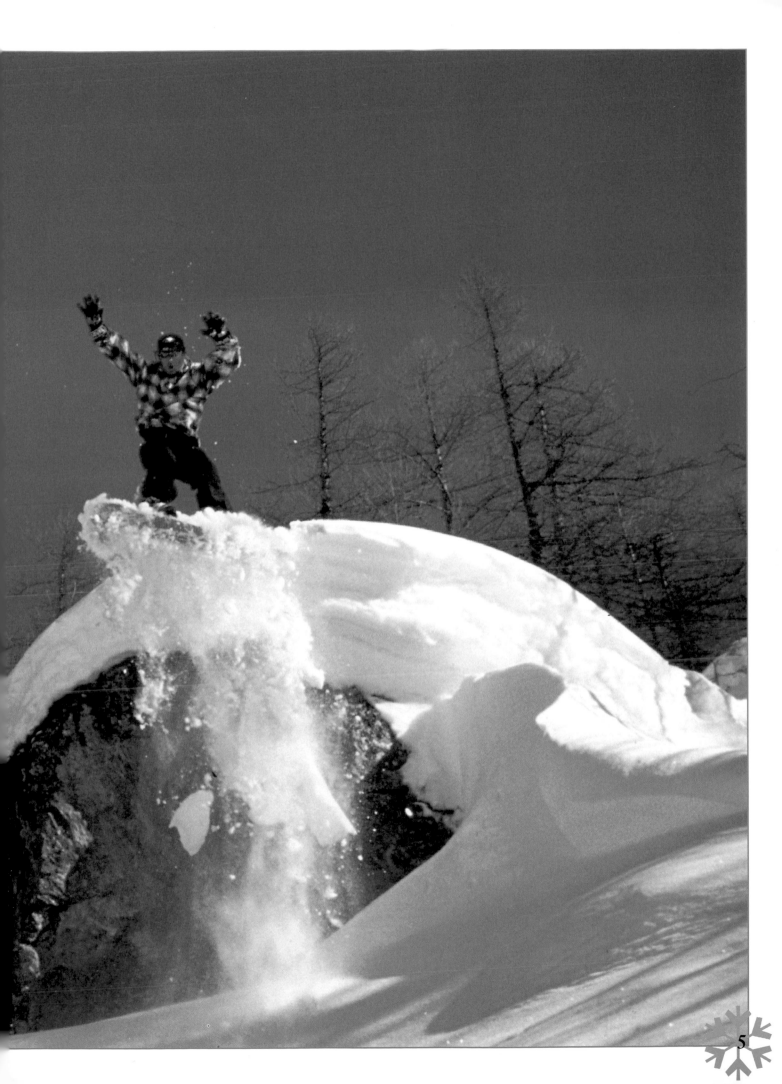

Getting into snowboarding

From freeriding to racing, there are several snowboarding styles — with new ones developing all the time. As a beginner, you need to learn the basic techniques and skills before you start experimenting with different styles.

Snowboarding is about feeling free and doing what you want to do in your own way, safely. Pick up your board, take along your sense of humor, and have fun!

FREERIDING

Freeriding gives you the best of every snowboarding style — you are free to choose from all of them! Freeriders make use of all the different types of snow and terrain, from deep powder — light, fluffy snow — to bumps and moguls (see page 32). As a freerider, you can ride fast, find a big jump, or just glide gently along a field of fresh snow.

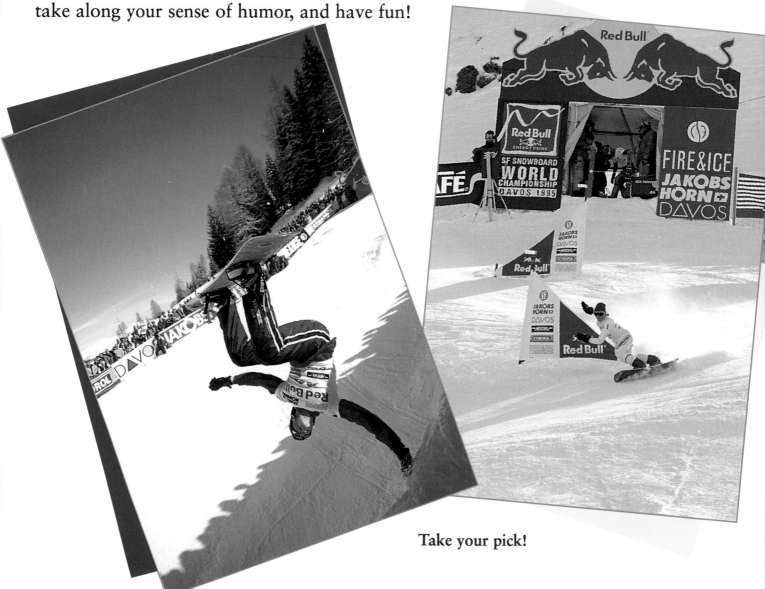

Take your pick!

In freestyle, snowboarders "catch air" and "pull tricks" in the park (an area with artificially built jumps) and the halfpipe (a channel carved out of the snow, above).

Racing (above) is a timed discipline in which riders try to pick the fastest line around "gates" or poles set in the snow.

FOLLOW THE SNOW

Many schools run trips to ski resorts where boarders are welcome. This can be a great opportunity to try out snowboarding. The best places to ride are in the large U.S. and Canadian ski resorts. Other places to ride include Argentina, Austria, Australia, Chile, France, Greece, Italy, New Zealand, Scotland, South Africa, Switzerland, and Turkey! Dry slopes, made of a material called Dendex, are very popular with beginners and experienced riders in Britain.

Extreme snowboarding (see pages 22 and 25) involves skill and courage as the rider tackles slopes and drops off the groomed trail (above).

SNURFING TO SNOWBOARDING

Snowboarding is only about 20 years old. It began when surfer Sherman Poppen designed a "snurfer," two skis bolted together, for surfing on snow, rather than water! Soon, snurf enthusiast Jake Burton changed the design of his snurfer, and the first basic snowboards began to hit the slopes. These early boards with foot straps were a long way from the high-tech equipment of today. As more and more people took their boards to the snow, the International Snowboard Federation (ISF) was set up as the worldwide governing body for the sport. Today, snowboarding is recognized as an Olympic sport.

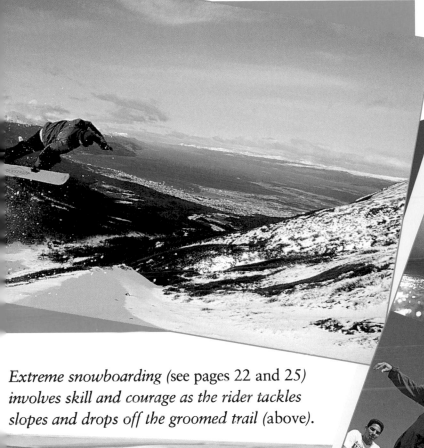

GETTING RELATED

Although its direct relation is the traditional sport of skiing (bottom right), snowboarding is known as an extreme sport — highly skillful but possibly dangerous — so safety is crucial. Other extreme sports that appeal particularly to young people are in-line skating, surfing (below left), BMX bike riding (below right), and skateboarding (bottom left). Snowboarding has been described as skateboarding or surfing on snow!

BINDING YOUR BOOTS

Soft boots (*right*) are the most popular. They are usually used with high-back bindings with two straps. These provide good ankle support. Many riders are now using step-in soft boots, which clip onto the board. Hard boots are used for racing.

Contact point

Nose or tip

Binding insert

Waist

Sidecut

Effective edge

View of the board from above

Shovel, or curve of the nose

Camber

View of the board from the side

STANCE WIDTH

Once you have decided whether you are goofy or regular (*see page 9*), you can set up your board with your stance width. This is the distance between the center points of your bindings (*right*). As a guide, your feet should be about shoulder-width apart but the best stance width is really the one that feels most comfortable for you. If your stance is too wide, you cannot turn; if it is too narrow, you will not have good balance.

Binding inserts allow you to adjust the stance width.

Once you have found a comfortable width, you need to set the angles (right). Most freeriders and freestylers ride with between 10° and 30° on the front foot and 3° to 15° on the back foot.

BASIC BOARD FACTS

The nose, or tip, and tail of the board curve up, allowing the board to float over the snow. The "effective edges" are the sharp metal edges that are in contact with the snow. The waist of the board gives the sidecut, the curve of the board's edge. A small waist means a quicker turn.

Contact point

Binding insert

Tail

Tail kick, or curve of the tail

inding inserts allow you to adjust the stance angle.

Boarding equipment

There are many different types and brands of boards and boots — but don't panic. As a beginner, start with soft boots with high-back bindings and use a freeride/freestyle board. The bindings, which can be adjusted, secure your boots to the board. With this set up, you can enjoy all kinds of riding, on all kinds of snow.

If, after awhile, you want to specialize in one kind of riding, such as racing, you can then change your equipment.

REGULAR OR GOOFY?

If you snowboard with your left foot forward, or leading, (the one closest to the board's tip or nose) you are regular (*left*); if you snowboard with your right foot forward, you are goofy (*below*).

To find out if you are regular or goofy, ask a friend to push you gently forward. Whichever foot you put down to steady yourself is your leading or front foot, and should be the one leading on your board.

DO YOUR BOOTS FIT?

Whether you are hiring boots or buying them, take your time. They need to fit well for comfort and skillful riding.

Your boots should feel comfortable, like sneakers. You want to be able to wiggle your toes, but you should not be able to lift up your heels.

It is a good idea to take a pair of ski socks to put on when you buy or rent boots.

Clothing for safety and comfort

Snowboarding is about style so it is important to look good as well as to feel comfortable and be safe. There are many styles of snowboard clothing to choose from. You will need warm, waterproof clothing to keep you dry and warm.

Accessories such as goggles aren't just there to look good — they are there for safety and protection.

HOW'S YOUR HEAD?

Snowboarding can be dangerous. Always wear a helmet when you are a beginner, and particularly in icy conditions. Even the most experienced riders wear helmets and most people wear them in the pipe and park (*see pages 34-35*). Not all shops sell snowboarding helmets for young people — an in-line skating helmet (*above*) or a mountain bike helmet will do just as well. Wear a wool hat for warmth underneath. With goggles (*above*), too, you can look pretty cool.

SUN SENSE

When you are high up in the mountains, your skin and eyes are exposed to strong sunlight, magnified by the glare from the snow. Sun rays can burn you, even when it is very cold. Apply some lip protection and cover your face with a high factor (20+) sunscreen or sunblock. This will also protect your skin from the wind and cold. Shield your eyes from the sun with a good pair of goggles or sunglasses.

UNDERNEATH...?

What you wear under your snowboarding clothes is important for comfort and warmth. If it is cold, wear many layers of light clothing that trap air to keep you warm, but that can also be removed if you get too hot. Natural fibers, such as cotton, stop you from sweating too much.

— *Inner gloves*

— *A fleece sweatshirt is light, warm, and durable. It also dries easily if it gets wet (which it probably will !)*

— *Leggings*

Warm socks are important.

10

Over a third of body heat is lost through your head. Cover it up!

...AND ON TOP?

Outerwear can be expensive, depending on the material it is made from. Gore-tex material is highly waterproof and durable — but very costly. There are many cheaper alternatives — look around to see what fits your needs and your price range.

Don't forget gloves, or mittens, and a hat. A neck warmer will also keep the cold out, especially when you take a tumble (*below*)!

WET, WET, WET!

Or rather dry, dry, dry! You will be a happier rider if you have waterproofed your outerwear (left), especially your boots and gloves, before you hit the slopes. Use a special waterproofing cream. You can also waterproof materials with a spray.

Pad yourself out with wrist guards and knee pads, or wear gloves with built-in wrist guards, and pants with built-in knee pads.

Most riders wear soft boots that are more flexible than hard boots.

11

What to do first

Snowboarding can be quite strenuous, so it is a good idea to get in shape before you take to the slopes (*see page 38 for your warm-up*). If your body is not used to the demands of the activity, you are more likely to injure yourself by pulling a muscle (placing too much strain on a muscle). Increase your fitness by playing different sports, from in-line skating to soccer.

Now, it is time to get to a ski slope — but it is important that you have a couple of lessons before setting off on your own.

LESSONS
Lessons are offered at most ski resorts. Make sure the instructor is fully certified with the American Association of Snowboarding Instructors (AASI) or the Professional Ski Instructors of America (PSIA).

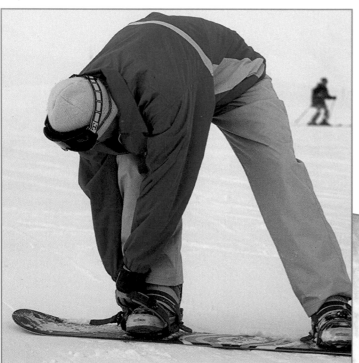

BOARDING UP

The easiest and safest way to put on your board is to attach the safety leash on your board to your front leg when you are standing. This stops the board from sliding down the slope, without you! You can then sit down, facing down the hill; put your front foot into your binding and fasten it up (*below*). Next, put your back foot into the binding and fasten it up. Some experienced riders prefer to attach their bindings from a standing position (*left*).

BINDINGS

If you have standard high-back bindings with two straps (*see page 8*), practice attaching and adjusting them. They can take a while to get used to! Be gentle with the clips, especially if it is cold because they will break if handled roughly. If they freeze up, take your board inside for ten minutes to defrost before using it. Check that all of the straps are well out of the way before putting your feet in, or you might break one.

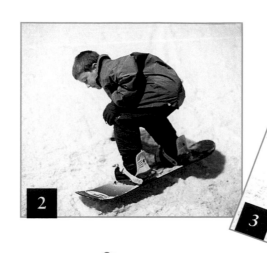

GET UP!

Once you have secured your leash and fastened your bindings while sitting down, you are ready to get up. First, practice this on flat ground.

Turn yourself around so you are facing up the hill. To do this, twist the board into the air and roll around its tail 1. Put your knees on the ground. It is then easy to push yourself up, using your hands 2. Be careful not to over-balance.

As soon as you are standing, you must find the balanced or "ready" position. Keep your knees slightly bent and your stomach muscles tense. Turn your shoulders and head to face the same way as your feet 3. The ready position is one of the most important positions to learn — you will use it both as a beginner and as an experienced rider.

Apart from the angle of your head, the ready position stays the same, even if you are riding fakie, or backward (*left*).

ARE YOU READY?
Before riding, check that:
❄ Your leash is attached.
❄ Your boots and bindings are secure.
❄ You are in the ready position.
❄ Now, off you go!

POSITION CHECK
By keeping your stomach muscles tight, you will help to maintain your balance. Keep your knees slightly bent.

This is your toe-side.

This is your toe-edge.

Slightly flex or tense your ankle joints.

This is your heel-side.

This is your heel-edge.

Falling down...

...backward (above)!

FALLING FAST

When you feel yourself over-balancing backward, bend your knees more, as if you are about to sit down (*left*). Only put your hands on the ground, protected by your wrist guards, when you have landed.

When you feel yourself over-balancing forward, move as if you are about to kneel down; put your knees down to help you break your fall — at this point you will feel the benefit of your knee pads. Finish the fall onto your forearms (*right*).

Going down... forward!

Go low to increase pressure (left).

Stand tall to reduce pressure (right).

Now that you are familiar with your equipment and the ready position, you can at last get moving, slowly! Make sure you have a good feel of the ready position (*see page 13*), know how to fall over, and how to get back up again (*see page 13*). Practice your pressure control technique (*left*) — this will not only help you to stop but it will also help you with more advanced moves (*see page 29*). Remember to wear your wrist guards and helmet, whether you are just learning or are an expert.

PRESSURE CONTROL

Practice changing the pressure of your weight on the base of your board (*above*). Stand tall to reduce the pressure; bend your knees and tense your legs to increase the pressure. Practice changing pressure from edge to edge. Stand still and rock from the toe-edge to the heel-edge on flat ground. Try lifting your toes up when on a heel-edge and pointing them down when on a toe-edge.

14

WANT A LIFT?
There are three main types of lifts at ski resorts to get you up the mountains — chair-lifts, T-bars, and gondolas. Gondolas are easy because you take your board off. The others take a bit of getting used to.

To get on and off a T-bar, as shown in the sequence (*right*), take your back foot out of your bindings.

SCOOTING ALONG

To get the feel of moving, practice scooting around on your board with your back foot out of your binding. Use your back foot to push, keeping your weight on your front foot (*left*). This must be done on flat ground!

Once you are confident with this, with both boots in the bindings, use pressure control to slide down a gentle slope. Try it on your toe-edge and then your heel-edge. Try the "falling leaf" exercise — move your weight onto your front foot and then your back foot when sliding slowly down the hill.

Even as you scoot, keep the ready position with your hands in front of you.

Grab the bar with your front hand and place it between your legs. Put your back foot between your bindings and distribute your weight more onto your back foot for takeoff. When you begin to move, stand up and even out your weight. To get off, take the lift from between your legs; let go with your front hand and glide to a stop.

STOP!
Stopping on your toe- or heel-edge is basically the same as a pressure control exercise. Practice by sliding down the hill on your toe- or heel-edge; then bend your knees to apply more pressure. This should bring you to a stop (above). Make sure you keep your weight slightly back, your hands forward, and your knees slightly bent.

15

SLALOM COURSE

A slalom run is a race course in which the gates are close together (*left*). As the racer goes toward the gate, he or she puts the board on an edge and presses hard, to make the board edge bite into the snow, creating a high speed carve (*see page 28*), close to the gate. A tight turn means a fast race. To protect themselves from the gates, as they whiz around them, racers wear protective padding and head and face gear.

BOOTS AND BOARDS
Racing snowboards, boots, and bindings allow the riders to make high-speed carves. The boards are thin and long. The boots (left) are hard, similar to ski boots. They are used with "plate" bindings that clip onto the toe and heel of the boot. Racers use steep angles on their stance, usually between 45° and 60°.

DEBORAH ANTHONIAZ
After only seven years racing, Deborah Anthoniaz became the ISF and FIS (*see page 17*) Junior World Champion in giant slalom (*see page 22*). Aged 19, she will now compete at senior level. Begin your racing by joining a club — they welcome all abilities.

Snowboard racing

In racing, speed is essential as riders are timed against the clock. They ride, between markers set in the snow, at incredible speeds — up to 50 miles per hour. This racing is known as running gates. To race, you need to be very precise and have excellent edge control to increase your speed.

Riders often train in the summer and fall, running gates on glaciers, huge areas of ice.

Getting Involved

There is a thriving network of competitions to challenge snowboarders of all levels and ages. As well as the Olympics and the International Snowboard Federation (ISF) competition, there is also a World Cup tour, run by the Federation Internationale de Ski (FIS).

Major competition events include the halfpipe (see page 19), boarder cross (see page 19), slalom, dual slalom, and giant slalom (see page 22). Other competitions feature big air (below), slope-style, and extreme snowboarding (see pages 19-21).

FROM SMALL BEGINNINGS
Many young riders begin their snowboarding careers by competing in events organized by their regional or national snowboarding association. These events can lead to entry in showcase competitions and events (above), where riders are invited to compete for cash prizes. A top-level rider will need to secure sponsorship to finance his or her training.

Begin at youth level (under 16 years old, above); from junior level (under 18 years), move on to the senior level.

JUST FOR FUN
Competitions aren't just about winning... although it's great if you do win. They're also about having fun (*left*), challenging yourself, and meeting other riders. Make sure any event you enter is suitable for your level.

In Training

Professional snowboarders work with skilled coaches to make the most of their talents. As with any other sport, the relationship the athlete has with his or her coach is very important. Riders must trust their coach totally if they are to do well. Even though professional snowboarders take their sport very seriously, snowboard teams have a very friendly atmosphere (*above left*).

Catching air!

A grab in the pipe!

Committed riders take part in other sports and physical activities to keep themselves in shape. Skills such as trampolining and gymnastics help them with their riding technique and skills.

Training doesn't just involve other physical sports such as surfing (above). Video analysis, when riders watch themselves on video, helps the riders to see what they are doing wrong, for future reference.

Racing to the finish.

Top-level snowboarders will train in a gym so they are at the peak of their fitness for the season.

Preparations

Some resots have supported snowboarding for years, holding regular competitive events. Today, many more resorts host snowboarding competitions. A resort usually needs to begin planning a year in advance of the competition.

Time for a slalom run!

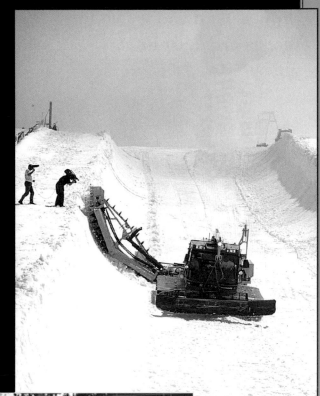

ARE YOU READY?
Before a competition, officials must check the race courses and organize the making of the halfpipes, usually carved out of the snow by special machines called pipe dragons (right).

Extremely brave!

Several riders tackle the boarder cross course at once.

Carving a halfpipe out by hand (left) is harder than using the pipe dragon.

SAFETY

Resorts have to consider the safety of the riders and the public when planning for an event. Special netting is put up around the race course and the halfpipe. The boarder cross course must be closed off to the public, in case of accidents.

At every competition the organizers must ensure that there is an emergency first aid and a rescue service on standby.

The public enjoys the events from a safe position (above).

Rules

To lessen the risk of injury to competitors and spectators, each event has its own strict rules. There are limits on the number of people allowed in the halfpipe at the same time for the warm-up and on the boarder cross at practice time. Riders have a set time to inspect a race course (*right*) and to practice (*left*).

FINI

RULED OUT

❅ *If you miss a gate in a racing event, you are disqualified. You are also disqualified if you run the gates (see page 16) during inspection time, when officials check the course.*

❅ *You will be disqualified if you ride the pipe at any time other than in your competition run or during the allowed practice period.*

❅ *If you fall on the first hit in a halfpipe event, you have two minutes to try again. After this time, you will be disqualified.*

❅ *If you go out of the boarder cross course during the competition, you will be disqualified.*

VIDEO TIME

Spectators are not allowed at the site of an extreme event. They must be content with watching video footage later, taken by someone with permission to accompany the competitors. For a good picture, photographers have to use long lens cameras (*below*).

A "roast beef" in the air (see page 30).

Extreme riding

Extreme snowboarding, or free-riding off-track in very difficult conditions, is exciting and exhilarating — but it can be very dangerous. The rider should be very skilled and experienced, and have the correct attitude, knowing his or her limits. An extreme rider always checks for avalanche danger and wears a special transmitter called a bleeper. High-pitched signals from this help the rescue services to find riders who are lost or buried in an avalanche.

CLIFF DROPS

For a successful cliff drop (*right*) the landing must be steep, fairly smooth, and soft. The run out (the flat area at the bottom of the slope) must be long enough to prevent the rider from hitting anything. The rider needs to have enough speed to clear any rocks.

AVALANCHES

Avalanches are set off if layers of snow are disturbed, causing heavy slabs of snow to hurtle down the mountain. They are more likely to happen on steep slopes after a heavy snowfall. Many resorts use dynamite to clear such potentially dangerous areas of snow.

CHUTES

As with cliffs, the extreme rider must check the entry and exit of the chute (a natural gulley, *left*), before attempting it. The steeper and narrower the chute, the faster the speed at the bottom and the longer the run out needed.

Up you go!
To climb a
hill with your
snowboard
on, turn
around so
you are facing
up the hill. Put both your hands
on the ground in front of you and
jump your feet up to meet them.
This is quite hard work! Alternatively,
release one foot from the bindings.
Lift the board with your other foot
and take a step, cutting the
toe-edge into the snow (above).

If you have a long way to go,
take your board off and walk!

THE FALL LINE

If you drop something at the top of a hill it will fall straight down the fall line — the direction that gravity pulls you down the hill (*right*). If you stand tall on your board and take the pressure off the edges, the board will go down the fall line.

TRAVERSING

The key to traversing (traveling across the hill, without losing too much height, *below*) is to turn your body the way you want to go. Keep in the ready position, with your hands in front of you. Flex your knee and ankle joints. Make sure that you are on an edge.

If you turn to face too much up or down the hill, you will "catch" an edge, and fall. This is when you are not clearly enough on an edge — the board becomes flat and the downhill edge digs into the snow — and over you go!

TIME FOR A TURN

For a basic turn (*above*), keep your back hand in front of your back foot. From the ready position, put some edge on, either heel- or toe-side, by lifting or pointing your toes.

Begin to glide down the fall line. Turn your head, arms, and shoulder in the direction that you want to travel in — the board will follow.

On the move

Once you have found your balance and come to grips with stopping and changing pressure, you can start to move at greater speeds. Soon you will be gliding, traversing (gliding across the fall line), and turning, down and along the slope. Slopes can get very busy with boarders and skiers; to avoid crashes, always be aware of the movements of other slope users.

2

1

Keep an edge or you will catch the opposite edge and fall.

SIDESLIPPING

Sideslipping — sliding down the fall line on one edge — will help control your speed and will improve your stopping skills. Begin in the ready position. Face up the hill and balance your weight evenly between your feet; gradually apply pressure so your toe-edge grips the snow 1 . To slide, straighten your legs slightly to release the edge grip, slowly flattening the board on the snow 2 . Increase the pressure on the toe-edge to slow down or stop. Practice sideslipping on your heel-edge and sideslipping at different speeds.

Twisting and Turning

If you are confident with traversing, sideslipping, and your basic turns, you are ready to try some toe-side and heel-side turns. Remember to begin from your ready position, with your hands in front of you. As you will be turning at greater speeds, it is advisable to wear your pads and a helmet to begin with. When you have conquered this turning technique you can try carving — an advanced turn in which the board does not slide but stays on its edge during the turn.

Keep your weight on one edge.

HEEL-SIDE TURN

Get some speed up by sideslipping down the hill, toe-edge. Keeping most of your weight on your front foot, lower your heels to flatten the board. Lift up your toes to bring the board onto the heel-edge. Start the turn by leaning slightly backward into the hill — don't sit down! Turn your upper body in the direction in which you want to turn and slide your back foot down the hill. As you feel the edge bite, press through your legs and follow the turn with your shoulders. As you complete the move, return to the sideslip position, heel-edge, ready for the toe-side turn.

MAKING THE LINK

To link turns, follow a heel-side turn immediately with a toe-side turn, as in the sequence pictured. Make sure that your shoulders follow the direction of your feet, from movement to movement. Move clearly from edge to edge — otherwise you will "catch" an edge and fall.

When you turn, and especially when you link turns, you need

to make sure that the way is clear. Always look where you are going!

Move to the opposite edge as you turn.

TOE-SIDE TURN

Build up some speed by sideslipping, heel-edge, down the hill. Transfer most of your weight over your front foot. Start the turn by slightly leaning into the hill with your shoulders. Flatten your board and you will feel it move down the fall line (*see page 26*). With your weight still mostly on your front foot, use your pressure skills (*see page 14*) to put your board onto the toe-edge. Don't twist your whole body, but turn your upper body to face toward the direction of the turn. Press through your legs and the board will follow the direction of your upper body.

Your board is now on the toe-edge.

STRAIGHT AIRS

For your first air, find a small jump with a smooth, gentle landing. Practice going over the jump without taking air first. When you feel more confident, approach, or hit, the jump a little faster, and ollie (*see below*) as you get to the top. Make sure that your board is not on an edge when you take off or you will become unbalanced in the air.

Once you are used to being in the air, try some grabs — different ways of holding the board while you are in the air. As you take off, reach down with your back hand and grab in between your feet, toe-edge — this is an "indie."

Style an air by "boning" it (left) — straightening one leg during a trick and holding the position while you are in the air.

OLLIEING

Before you learn to jump, you need to learn to ollie. This is a basic trick that propels you into the air, without using a launch or hit. Ollieing is a lot of fun and it's a great way to keep your balance on the board.

Before you ollie on a slope, practice on flat ground.

Start in your ready position, with your hands in front of you. Begin moving in a straight line. Rock your weight onto your back foot ☐1. Spring forward and up off the tail of your board ☐2.

Snowboarding trickery

Once you are confident and safe with the basic moves, you can try some tricks from airs to ollies. Before you start any trick or variation, remember to use your ready position — without it you are more likely to lose control when you land. Tricks also look cooler and more stylish if the rider seems to be in control, without his or her arms and hands waving all over the place!

As you develop your ability to perform tricks, you can start to polish your own style. Take a look at other more experienced riders and try to copy their moves — but only attempt what you can do safely. Make up your own tricks and moves — with names too!

FAKING IT OR SWITCHING IT? *Riding fakie is riding backward (tail first) or leading with the foot that usually follows. The technique for riding fakie is similar to that for riding forward (nose first), except that you twist more with your hips. Make sure that you are looking in the direction in which you want to travel, checking that there are no people or obstacles in your way. Try to keep your weight centered, without leaning too far forward. Practice riding fakie because it will help you later to learn some harder tricks. If you start a trick, such as an ollie (above), tail first, you are riding switch.*

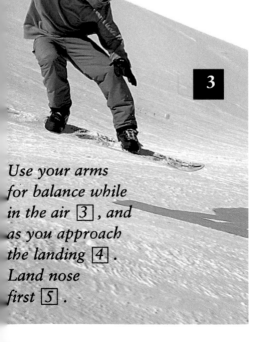

3

Use your arms for balance while in the air 3 *, and as you approach the landing* 4 *. Land nose first* 5 *.*

4

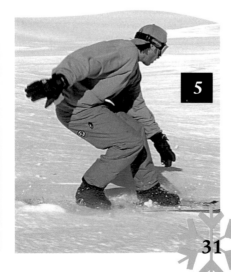

5

31

There are often lots of people on the slopes, from skiers to walkers. By observing certain "rules" everyone can enjoy themselves safely.

❋ Always look behind you before you set off.

❋ Never pass too close to another slope user.

❋ Only ever hit a jump when you are completely sure that the landing is clear.

❋ Always wait your turn before dropping in to hit a jump.

❋ Don't mess around on the lifts.

❋ Be polite and friendly to other slope users — and smile, it's more

Advanced freeriding

Freeriding is about finding the places you like to ride and experimenting with tricks that you can perform safely. When you are confident with freeriding on the trail (a groomed slope where the snow is packed), you may want to try some off-trail riding.

The snow on an off-trail slope is powder (*see right*). Here you will find the most difficult runs on the mountain. Different types of snow mean that places will be better at different times during the season and the day. On-trail, or off-trail, always be aware of other slope users. Never ride fast in a beginners' area or if it is very busy.

BUMPING AND SPEEDING

Freeriding at high speeds (right) is also a lot of fun, especially if the trail has just been groomed. Try some high-speed carves. Feel your edges biting into the snow. Put more angle on your stance (see page 8) — this will make the edges hold even better.

Bumps and moguls are a lot of fun if the snow is very mushy, but are terrible if it is icy. A mogul is a large bump in the snow created when many people have turned in the same place. The easiest way to ride them is to turn in the gaps between each bump.

OFF-TRAIL

Riding off-trail is one the greatest challenges, even for the most experienced snowboarder.

Only ever attempt to go off-trail when you are a competent and confident rider. Never go alone and always tell an adult where you are going, and at what time you expect to be back. Before going off-trail in the mountains check with the ski patrol if it is safe to do so. When you begin, look for snow that is approximately a boot's depth — any deeper and you may find it more work than fun!

Some experienced snowboarders enjoy off trail riding in between the trees (above). This is fairly dangerous, so they do not attempt this at great speeds or when the snow is hard.

POWDER

Powder snow is fresh, deep, light, and dry — riding it is every boarder's dream. It is easy to do as long as you remember to keep your weight on your back foot. It is also a good idea to set your bindings back from the center of your board so you do not sink in the snow. There is nothing better than seeing a wide-open powder field with no tracks — and making the field your own (above).

33

Parks and pipes

Parks and pipes are areas created for snowboarders to practice and learn new tricks. A park (*main image*) consists of large jumps, kickers, table tops, spines, and gaps, all of which are made out of compacted snow. The pipe is a shaped slope, like a pipe cut in half or a quarter. Perfect the tricks you already know and learn some new ones. Be inspired by more experienced riders — but don't be intimidated by them. They were beginners once, too!

SPINES
Learn tricks and invent your own on a spine. A spine is a ridge or rail on which tricks can be performed.

TABLE TOPS
On a table top there is a takeoff, a landing, and a top over which you jump. Make sure you have enough speed to make the landing. Experiment with straight airs and grabs (see pages 30), such as the "indie," on a table top (above).

Advanced riders can try spins — 180° at first, then 360°. Turn your head and spot your landing — focus on the point where you intend to land.

IN THE PIPE

When you ride the pipe (above and right), don't worry about catching air from the walls — jumping from the sides. Begin by smoothly riding the transition (the curved area) to get used to the feel of the pipe. Ride to the top of the wall before turning around to jump back down again. Once you have the hang of this, increase your speed so that you can get some air, then try a few grabs!

GAPS

These are like boxes, except there is a gap instead of a flattened area (left). When you jump them, you must make sure that you have enough speed or you will miss the landing and fall down the gap. Only jump a gap if you are sure you can clear it!

STAY SAFE

Parks and pipes are fun, but unless you are fully protected and ride safely, you could injure yourself and others.

❄ Wear pads, guards, and a helmet.

❄ Be safe, and polite — always wait your turn before dropping into the pipe or park.

❄ Unless you are landing, stay clear of landing areas.

Care of your snowboard

It is very important to take proper care of your kit, especially your board. Don't bang it on the ground to remove snow — brush it off.

When you are using your board, have it waxed at a workshop in a store or resort at least once a week, to prevent the base from drying out.

[1] The base of the board is cleaned with some wax remover.

[2] The edges are smoothed with a file. This file is quite sharp so care must be taken when using it.

[3] Once the side edges are fairly smooth, they are sharpened with a file.

Using a file guide ensures that the edges are evenly filed.

[4] A metal brush or a scourer (above) is used to remove any filings left over.

[5] Small holes can be filled with a substance called P-Tex. This is lighted using a candle and dripped into the hole. P-Tex can burn your skin, so always be careful if you are in a workshop or near someone using P-Tex. The board is now ready for repair.

[6] In the workshop, a special gun is used to melt the P-Tex into the hole in the snowboard.

[7] The technician checks to see if the P-Tex has filled in the hole.

[8] Any excess P-Tex is removed by filing the base smooth with a fine file.

[9] With the wax iron on a medium setting, wax is melted onto the board.

With regular waxing, your board will last longer and you will be able to ride faster.

10 *The wax is ironed into the board ensuring even coverage. The iron is never left to rest on the base at any time.*

11 *Any excess wax is scraped off with a plastic scraper when the wax is cool.*

12 *The base of the board is then treated with a scratch pad to create small grooves in the wax on the board. As tiny drops of water move along the base of the board, it is easier for the board to go faster along the snow.*

Snowboard accessories

You will be able to find any accessories you might need in a good snowboard store or via mail order through snowboard magazines. Special accessories, like avalanche bleeper, will have to be ordered from the manufacturer or bought at a good mountaineering shop.

STREET GEAR

There are many inexpensive street-wear clothes to be found with snowboard influences. As snowboarding is a very close relative of skateboarding, many companies make both skate- and snowboard wear. This means snowboarders can look good both on and off the slope (*below*).

To find a good selection of the latest street wear, visit your nearest skateboard or snowboard store. Cool street wear means wearing clothes you feel comfortable in — don't be scared to be a bit different!

IN YOUR POCKET
Pocket-sized tools are ideal to take up the mountain, in case you need to tighten your bindings. Take a water bottle with you, too.

Safety on the slopes

Snowboarding can be dangerous. The mountains are very beautiful but full of hazards. Always be aware of the basic ways in which you can cut down the risk of injury to yourself and others. Remember that you can combine good mountain awareness and a sense of safety with the fun of snowboarding.

WARMING UP
Warm up with stretches before riding. Hold each stretch for 10 seconds. Include all parts of your body (*left*). Ask a gym teacher or your instructor for further advice.

DON'T FORGET! ALWAYS…
❄ Warm up thoroughly.
❄ Wear full protective clothing.
❄ Tell an adult where you are going and how long you will be.
❄ Check the weather forecast — don't go out in bad weather.
❄ Organize a time and place if you are meeting someone.
❄ In a new area, take a trail map.
❄ Have good mountain awareness.
❄ Don't go on slopes that are too difficult for you — stay safe.
❄ Be courteous… and have fun!

ALL SIGNED UP
Try to remember the colors and shapes of the track markers (*right*), as well as the danger and warning signs. These signs are used in all resorts as well as on trail maps. A trail map is an easy-to-follow representation of the trails on the mountain and of any dangerous areas.

Safety signs and markers indicate the degree of difficulty of a run and alert you to any dangers. Only attempt a run that you know you can safely handle.

○ *Very easy*

□ *Intermediate*

Difficult ◇

◇ ◇ *Very difficult*

Avalanche warning

Warning signs

Crossing

SLOW
Warning sign

Snowboard Speak

Air A jump.

Binding An attachment that secures the boot to the board.

Bleeper A transmitter that makes a bleeping noise.

Boarder cross A competition course that includes obstacles.

Bumps Raised areas in the snow.

Carve A high-speed turn, in which the board stays on an edge.

Dendex The plastic material from which dry slopes are made.

Dual slalom Like a slalom, but two riders compete head-to-head.

Edge A side of the board that comes in contact with the snow.

Extreme An extreme sport involves skill and danger. Extreme snowboarding involves cliff jumps in the most challenging terrain.

Fakie Riding backward or with the leading leg following.

Flex To contract or tighten.

Freeriding A snowboarding style that includes all styles.

Freestyle A snowboarding style in which the rider catches air and rides the pipe.

Gap A table top with a gap in the middle over which you jump.

Giant slalom A long, timed race in which the markers are farther apart than on a slalom.

Goofy Snowboarding with your right foot forward.

Grab Arm and leg variations on a move.

Halfpipe A halfpipe shaped channel carved out in the snow.

Heel-edge The edge of the board on your heel-side.

Heel-side The side of your board behind your heels.

Hit Approaching a jump, or another word for a jump.

Kicker A steep jump.

Ollieing A launch into the air without using a jump.

P-Tex A material for mending holes in your board.

Park An area for boarders with jumps and tricks.

Pipe A half- or quarterpipe shape, carved out in the snow.

Pulling tricks Doing stunts or special moves on a snowboard.

Quarterpipe A quarterpipe shaped channel carved out in the snow.

Racing Snowboarding against the clock.

Regular Snowboarding with your left foot forward.

Slalom A timed race through a set of markers or gates.

Slope-style A competition event that includes jumps and quarterpipes.

Spine A ridge or rail on which you can perform tricks.

Stance angle The angle at which you set your bindings.

Stance width The distance between your bindings.

Switch Performing a trick, such as an ollie, backward.

Table top A raised area of snow over which riders can jump and perform tricks.

Terrain The type of land over which you ride.

Toe-edge The edge of the board on your toe-side.

Toe-side The side of your board in front of your toes.

Index

Photo Credits: *Abbreviations: t-top, m-middle, b-bottom, r-right, l-left*

All the pictures in this book were supplied by Snowboarding UK magazine except for the following: pages 1, 4-5, 7 all, 18ml & bl, 25t, 32b, 32-33 & 33 – Frank Spooner Pictures; 2, 3, 8tm, 10, 11l, 12t & b, 14t, 26tl, 36-37 all & 38 – Roger Vlitos.

The publishers would like to thank the Tamworth Snowdome, Boardwise in Chiswick, Boardwise in Tamworth and Snowboarding UK for their help and cooperation in the preparation of this book.